·*Cooking for Today*·

LOW-FAT COOKING

·*Cooking for Today*·

LOW-FAT COOKING

KATHRYN HAWKINS

A Siena Book
Siena is an imprint of Parragon Books

First published in Great Britain in 1996 by
Parragon Book Service Ltd
Unit 13-17
Avonbridge Trading Estate
Atlantic Road
Avonmouth
Bristol BS11 9QD

ISBN 0-7525-1570-5

Produced by Haldane Mason, London

Printed in Italy

Acknowledgements:
Art Direction: Ron Samuels
Editor: Michael Williams
Series Design: Pedro & Frances Prá-Lopez/Kingfisher Design
Page Design: Somewhere Creative
Photography: Amanda Heywood
Home Economist: Kathryn Hawkins

Saucepans supplied by Meyer Cookware UK
Photographs on pages 6, 20, 34, 48, 62: reproduced by permission of
ZEFA Picture Library (UK) Ltd.

Note:
Cup measurements in this book are for American cups. Tablespoons are assumed to be 15 ml.
Unless otherwise stated, milk is assumed to be full-fat, eggs are standard size 3 and pepper
is freshly ground black pepper.

Contents

CHAPTER ONE

Soups, Starters & Light Meals

Whether you're looking for a tasty meal opener or just a light supper, a lot of familiar dishes are full of fat. Here is a selection of appetizing low-fat recipes to suit all tastes.

The traditional way to open a meal is with a soup, such as Thai-style Chicken & Coconut Soup or Spicy Lentil Soup, although these can be meals in themselves. The key to successful soup-making has to be homemade stock. Ready-made stocks in the form of cubes and granules often contain large quantities of salt and flavourings, which can dominate a dish and overpower delicate flavours. Although it does take extra time to make your own stock, it's well worth it and if you make more than you need, it can easily be frozen in smaller, more usable quantities.

If you prefer something other than soup, then try toasted Bruschetta with sun-dried tomatoes and Mozzarella, or a mouth-watering Gazpacho Water Ice made from tasty vegetables.

Opposite: *Fresh vegetables can make delicious, warming soups, ideal for the low-fat diet.*

STEP 1

STEP 2

STEP 3

STEP 4

THAI-STYLE CHICKEN & COCONUT SOUP

This fragrant soup combines citrus flavours with coconut and a hint of piquancy from chillies.

SERVES: 4
PREPARATION: 19 MINS,
COOKING: 15 MINS

CALS/KJ PER PORTION: 284/1194
FAT PER PORTION: 14.4 G

350 g/12 oz/1¾ cups cooked, skinned
 chicken breast
125 g/4 oz/1⅓ cups unsweetened
 desiccated coconut
500 ml/16 fl oz/2 cups boiling water
500 ml/16 fl oz/2 cups Fresh Chicken
 Stock (see page 76)
4 spring onions (scallions), white and green
 parts, sliced thinly
2 stalks lemon grass
1 lime
1 tsp grated ginger root
1 tbsp light soy sauce
2 tsp ground coriander
2 large fresh red chillies
1 tbsp chopped fresh coriander (cilantro)
1 tbsp cornflour (cornstarch) mixed with
 2 tbsp cold water
salt and white pepper
chopped red chilli to garnish

1 Slice the chicken into thin strips.
Place the coconut in a heatproof
bowl and pour the boiling water over.

2 Place a fine sieve (strainer) over
another bowl and pour in the
coconut water. Work the coconut
through the sieve (strainer). Pour the
coconut water into a large saucepan and
add the stock.

3 Add the spring onions (scallions) to
the saucepan. Slice the base of each
lemon grass and discard damaged leaves.
Bruise the stalks and add to the saucepan.

4 Peel the rind from the lime, keeping
it in large strips. Slice the lime in
half and extract the juice. Add the lime
strips, juice, ginger, soy sauce and
ground coriander to the saucepan.

5 Bruise the chillies with a fork then
add to the saucepan. Heat the pan
to just below boiling point.

6 Add the chicken and fresh
coriander to the saucepan, bring to
the boil, then simmer for 10 minutes.

7 Discard the lemon grass, lime rind
and chillies. Pour the blended
cornflour (cornstarch) mixture into the
saucepan and stir until slightly
thickened. Season to taste then serve,
garnished with chopped red chilli.

SPICY LENTIL SOUP

For a warming, satisfying meal on a cold day, this lentil dish is packed full of taste and goodness.

STEP 2

STEP 3

STEP 4

STEP 5

SERVES: 4
PREPARATION: 10 MINS,
    COOKING 1 HR 10 MINS

CALS/KJ PER PORTION: 272/1141
FAT PER PORTION: 3 G

125 g/4 oz/¹/₂ cup red lentils
2 tsp vegetable oil
1 large onion, chopped finely
2 garlic cloves, crushed
1 tsp ground cumin
1 tsp ground coriander
1 tsp garam masala
2 tbsp tomato purée (paste)
1 litre/1³/₄ pints/4¹/₂ cups Fresh Vegetable
    Stock (see page 77)
about 350 g/12 oz can sweetcorn, drained
salt and pepper

TO SERVE:
low-fat natural yogurt
chopped fresh parsley
warmed pitta (pocket) bread

1 Rinse the lentils in cold water, drain well and set aside.

2 Heat the oil in a large non-stick saucepan and fry the onion and garlic gently until softened but not browned.

3 Stir in the cumin, coriander, garam masala, tomato purée (paste) and 4 tablespoons of the stock. Mix well and simmer gently for 2 minutes.

4 Add the lentils and pour in the remaining stock. Bring to the boil, reduce the heat and simmer, covered, for 1 hour until the lentils are tender and the soup thickened.

5 Stir in the sweetcorn and heat through for 5 minutes. Season well.

6 Ladle into warmed soup bowls and top each with a spoonful of yogurt and a sprinkling of parsley. Serve accompanied with warmed pitta (pocket) bread.

NOTE

Many of the ready-prepared ethnic breads available today either contain fat or are brushed with oil before baking. Always check the ingredients list for fat content.

STEP 2

STEP 3

STEP 4

STEP 5

POTATO SKINS WITH GUACAMOLE DIP

Although avocados do contain fat, if they are used in small quantities with the right balance of ingredients, you can still enjoy their creamy texture.

SERVES: 4
PREPARATION: 50 MINS,
  COOKING: 1 HR 40 MINS

CALS/KJ PER PORTION: 442/1856
FAT PER PORTION: 12 G

4 × 250 g/8 oz baking potatoes
2 tsp olive oil
coarse sea salt and pepper
chopped fresh chives to garnish

GUACAMOLE DIP:
175 g/6 oz ripe avocado
1 tbsp lemon juice
2 ripe, firm tomatoes, chopped finely
1 tsp grated lemon rind
100 g/ 3 1/2 oz/ 1/2 cup medium-fat soft cheese
  with herbs and garlic
4 spring onions (scallions), chopped finely
a few drops of Tabasco sauce
salt and pepper

1 Bake the potatoes directly on the oven shelf in a preheated oven at 200°C/400°F/Gas Mark 6 for 1 1/4 hours until tender. Remove from the oven and allow to cool for 30 minutes. Reset the oven to 220°C/425°F/Gas Mark 7.

2 Halve the potatoes lengthwise and scoop out 2 tablespoons of the flesh from the middle of each potato. Slice in half again. Place on a baking sheet and brush the flesh side lightly with oil. Sprinkle with salt and pepper. Bake for a further 25 minutes until golden and crisp.

3 Meanwhile make the guacamole dip. Halve the avocado and discard the stone (pit). Peel off the skin and mash the flesh with the lemon juice.

4 Transfer to a large bowl and mix with the remaining ingredients. Cover and chill until required.

5 Drain the potato skins on paper towels and transfer to a warmed serving platter. Garnish with chives. Pile the avocado mixture into a serving bowl.

TIPS

Mash the leftover potato flesh with natural yogurt and seasoning, and spoon on to meat, fish and vegetable fillings.

BRUSCHETTA

Traditionally, this Italian savoury is enriched with spoonfuls of olive oil. Here, sun-dried tomatoes are a good substitute and only a small amount of oil is used.

STEP 1

SERVES: 4
PREPARATION: 32 MINS,
    COOKING: 6 MINS

CALS/KJ PER PORTION: 294/1235
FAT PER PORTION: 6.3 G

60 g/2 oz/¼ cup dry-pack sun-dried
    tomatoes
300 ml/½ pint/1¼ cups boiling water
35 cm/14 inch long Granary or wholemeal
    (whole wheat) stick of French bread
1 large garlic clove, halved
30 g/1 oz/¼ cup pitted black olives in brine,
    drained and quartered
2 tsp olive oil
2 tbsp chopped fresh basil
45 g/1½ oz/⅓ cup grated low fat Italian
    Mozzarella cheese
salt and pepper
fresh basil leaves to garnish

1 Place the sun-dried tomatoes in a heatproof bowl and pour over the boiling water. Set aside for 30 minutes to soften. Drain well and pat dry with paper towels. Slice into thin strips and set aside.

2 Trim and discard the ends from the bread and cut into 12 slices. Arrange on a grill (broiler) rack and place under a preheated hot grill (broiler)

and cook for 1–2 minutes on each side until lightly golden.

3 Rub both sides of each piece of bread with the cut sides of the garlic. Top with strips of sun-dried tomato and olives.

4 Brush lightly with olive oil and season well. Sprinkle with the basil and Mozzarella cheese and return to the grill (broiler) for 1–2 minutes until the cheese is melted and bubbling. Transfer to a warmed serving platter and garnish with fresh basil.

VARIATIONS

Sun-dried tomatoes give a rich, full flavour to this dish, but thinly sliced fresh tomatoes can be used instead.

Use dry packed sun-dried tomatoes, as these have no added oil. If the only type available are packed in oil, drain them, rinse well in warm water and drain again on paper towels to remove as much oil as possible.

For a more substantial meal, place a thin slice of lean ham or a few flakes of tuna fish on top of the tomato.

STEP 2

STEP 3

STEP 4

STEP 1

STEP 2

STEP 5

STEP 6

TUNA & ANCHOVY PATE WITH MELBA CROUTONS

An excellent tangy combination which can be used for a sandwich filling or as a dip. The pâté will keep well in the refrigerator for up to one week.

SERVES: 6
PREPARATION: 1 HR 15 MINS,
  COOKING: 26 MINS

CALS/KJ PER PORTION: 168/704
FAT PER PORTION: 5.2 G

PATE:
50 g/1³/₄ oz can anchovy fillets, drained
about 400 g/13 oz can tuna fish in brine,
  drained
175 g/6 oz/³/₄ cup half-fat cottage cheese
125 g/4 oz/¹/₂ cup skimmed milk soft cheese
1 tbsp horseradish relish
¹/₂ tsp grated orange rind
white pepper

MELBA CROUTONS:
4 slices, thick sliced wholemeal
  (wholewheat) bread

TO GARNISH:
orange slices
fresh dill sprigs

1 To make the pâté, separate the anchovy fillets and pat well with paper towels to remove all traces of oil.

2 Place the anchovy fillets and remaining pâté ingredients into a blender or food processor. Blend for a few seconds until smooth. Alternatively, finely chop the anchovy fillets and flake the tuna, then beat together with the remaining ingredients; this will make a more textured pâté.

3 Transfer to a mixing bowl, cover and chill for 1 hour.

4 To make the melba croûtons, place the bread slices under a preheated medium grill (broiler) for 2–3 minutes on each side until lightly browned.

5 Using a serrated knife, slice off the crusts and slide the knife between the toasted edges of the bread.

6 Stamp out circles using a 5 cm/ 2 inch round cutter and place on a baking sheet. Alternatively, cut each piece of toast in half diagonally. Bake in a preheated oven at 150°C/300°F/Gas Mark 2 for 15–20 minutes until curled and dry.

7 Spoon the pâté on to serving plates and garnish with orange slices and fresh dill sprigs. Serve with the freshly baked melba croûtons.

STEP 1

STEP 2

STEP 4

STEP 5

GAZPACHO WATER ICE

Try serving this refreshing appetizer at a dinner party – it's certain to impress and contains virtually no fat.

SERVES: 4
PREPARATION: 20 MINS

CALS/KJ PER PORTION: 35/146
FAT PER PORTION: 0.5 G

500 g/1 lb/4 tomatoes
about 600 ml/1 pint/2½ cups boiling water
4 spring onions (scallions), chopped
2 celery sticks, chopped
1 small red (bell) pepper, chopped
1 garlic clove, crushed
1 tbsp tomato purée (paste)
1 tbsp chopped fresh parsley
salt and pepper
fresh parsley sprigs to garnish

TO SERVE:
shredded iceberg lettuce
bread sticks

1 Prick the skin of the tomatoes with a fork at the stalk end and place in a large heatproof bowl. Pour over enough boiling water to cover them. Leave for 5–10 minutes. After this time, the skin should start peeling away from the flesh. Leave for longer if necessary.

2 Skewer the tomatoes with a fork and peel away the skin. Slice the tomatoes in half, scoop out the seeds and discard. Chop the flesh.

3 Place the chopped tomatoes, spring onions (scallions), celery, (bell) pepper, garlic and tomato purée (paste) in a food processor or blender. Blend for a few seconds until smooth. Alternatively, finely chop or mince the vegetables then mix with the tomato purée (paste). Pour into a freezerproof container and freeze.

4 Remove from the freezer and leave at room temperature for 30 minutes. Break up with a fork and place in a blender or food processor. Blend for a few seconds to break up the ice crystals and form a smooth mixture. Alternatively, break up with a fork and beat with a wooden spoon until smooth.

5 Transfer to a mixing bowl and stir in the parsley and seasoning. Return to the freezer container and freeze for a further 30 minutes.

6 Fork through the water ice again and serve with shredded iceberg lettuce and bread sticks, and garnish with parsley.

VARIATIONS

This recipe is also excellent served unfrozen as a chilled soup: simply blend all the ingredients together and chill well before serving with ice cubes.

CHAPTER TWO

Fish & Shellfish Dishes

White fish and shellfish are naturally low in fat, so they are ideal to include in the diet. The different varieties of fish vary in texture and flavour and therefore lend themselves to assorted cooking methods, as we see in the recipes in the following chapter.

Bass, cod, coley, haddock, halibut, monkfish, mullet (red and grey), skate, sole (Dover and lemon), turbot and whiting are some of the most popular and readily available white fish found in the fishmonger's today. Rich in minerals and proteins, these fish have a very important role to play in the low-fat diet.

Oily fish – like salmon, trout, anchovy and tuna – are rich in fat-soluble vitamins A and D and the mineral calcium (where the bones are small enough to be eaten), and should only be consumed in small quantities. Although high in fat, it is now believed that the oils in oily fish could be beneficial in breaking down cholesterol in the bloodstream.

Opposite: *Shellfish are low in fat, rich in flavour and can be cooked in a variety of ways to produce mouthwatering low-fat meals.*

STEP 1

STEP 2

STEP 3

STEP 4

SMOKED FISH & CRAB CHOWDER

Packed full of flavour, this delicious fish dish is a meal in itself, but it is ideal accompanied with a crisp side salad.

SERVES: 4
PREPARATION: 15 MINS,
  COOKING: 27 MINS

CALS/KJ PER PORTION: 310/1303
FAT PER PORTION: 2.6 G

1 large onion, chopped finely
2 celery sticks, chopped finely
150 ml/¼ pint/⅔ cup dry white wine
600 ml/1 pint/2½ cups Fresh Fish Stock
  (see page 78)
600 ml/1 pint/2½ cups skimmed milk
1 dried bay leaf
250 g/8 oz/1½ cups smoked cod fillets,
  skinned and cut into 2.5 cm/1 inch cubes
250 g/8 oz undyed smoked haddock fillets,
  skinned and cut into 2.5 cm/1 inch cubes
2 × 175 g/6 oz cans crab meat, drained
250 g/8 oz blanched French (green) beans,
  sliced into 2.5 cm/1 inch pieces
250 g/8 oz/1½ cups cooked brown rice
4 tsp cornflour (cornstarch) mixed with
  4 tablespoons cold water
salt and pepper
chopped fresh parsley to garnish
mixed green salad to serve

1 Place the onion, celery and wine in a large non-stick saucepan. Bring to the boil, cover and cook for 5 minutes. Remove the lid and cook for a further 5 minutes until the liquid has evaporated.

2 Pour in the stock and milk and add the bay leaf. Bring to a simmer and stir in the cod and haddock. Simmer gently, uncovered, for 5 minutes.

3 Add the crab meat, French (green) beans and rice and cook gently for 2–3 minutes until heated through. Remove the bay leaf with a perforated spoon.

4 Stir in the cornflour (cornstarch) mixture until thickened slightly. Season to taste and ladle into 4 warmed soup bowls. Garnish with chopped parsley and serve with a mixed salad.

TIPS

Look out for undyed smoked fish at your fishmonger or supermarket; they are now available alongside the more familiar strongly coloured fish.

MEDITERRANEAN-STYLE FISH STEW

Popular in fishing ports around Europe, gentle stewing is an excellent way to maintain the flavour and succulent texture of fish and shellfish.

STEP 2

STEP 3

STEP 4

STEP 5

SERVES: 4
PREPARATION: 2 HRS 30 MINS,
  COOKING: 25 MINS

CALS/KJ PER PORTION: 358/1504
FAT PER PORTION: 7.1 G

2 tsp olive oil
2 red onions, sliced
2 garlic cloves, crushed
2 tbsp red wine vinegar
2 tsp caster (superfine) sugar
300 ml/¹/₂ pint/1¹/₄ cups Fresh Fish Stock
  (see page 78)
300 ml/¹/₂ pint/1¹/₄ cups dry red wine
2 × about 400 g/13 oz cans chopped
  tomatoes
250 g/8 oz baby aubergines (eggplant),
  quartered
250 g/8 oz yellow courgettes (zucchini),
  sliced
1 green (bell) pepper, sliced
1 tbsp chopped fresh rosemary
500 g/1 lb halibut fillet, skinned and cut
  into 2.5 cm/1 inch cubes
750 g/1¹/₂ lb fresh mussels, prepared
250 g/8 oz baby squid, cleaned, trimmed
  and sliced into rings
250 g/8 oz fresh tiger prawns (shrimp),
  peeled and deveined
salt and pepper
lemon wedges

4 slices toasted French bread rubbed with a
  cut garlic clove

1 Heat the oil in a large non-stick saucepan and fry the onions and garlic gently for 3 minutes.

2 Stir in the vinegar and sugar and cook for a further 2 minutes. Stir in the stock, wine, canned tomatoes, aubergines (eggplant) courgettes (zucchini), (bell) pepper and rosemary. Bring to the boil and simmer, uncovered, for 10 minutes.

3 Add the halibut, mussels and squid. Mix well and simmer, covered, for 5 minutes until the fish is opaque.

4 Stir in the prawns (shrimp) and continue to simmer, covered, for a further 2–3 minutes until the prawns (shrimp) are pink and cooked through.

5 Discard any mussels which haven't opened and season to taste. To serve, put a slice of the prepared garlic bread in the base of each warmed serving bowl and ladle the stew over the top. Serve with lemon wedges.

STEP 1

STEP 2

STEP 3

STEP 4

MUSSEL & SCALLOP SPAGHETTI

Juicy mussels and scallops poached gently in white wine are the perfect accompaniment to pasta to make a sophisticated meal.

SERVES: 4
PREPARATION: 2 HRS 15 MINS,
  COOKING: 27 MINS

CALS/KJ PER PORTION: 411/1727
FAT PER PORTION: 9.4 G

250 g/8 oz dried wholemeal (wholewheat)
  spaghetti
60 g/2 oz/2 slices rindless lean back bacon,
  chopped
2 shallots, chopped finely
2 celery stick, chopped finely
150 ml/¼ pint/⅔ cup dry white wine
150 ml/¼ pint/⅔ cup Fresh Fish Stock (see
  page 78)
500 g/1 lb fresh mussels, prepared
250 g/8 oz shelled queen or China bay
  scallops
1 tbsp chopped fresh parsley
salt and pepper

1 Cook the spaghetti in a saucepan of boiling water according to the packet instructions, until the pasta is cooked but 'al dente', firm to the bite – about 10 minutes.

2 Meanwhile, gently dry-fry the bacon in a large non-stick frying pan (skillet) for 2–3 minutes. Stir in the shallots, celery and wine. Simmer gently, uncovered, for 5 minutes until softened.

3 Add the stock, mussels and scallops, cover and cook for a further 6–7 minutes. Discard any mussels that remain unopened.

4 Drain the spaghetti and add to the frying pan (skillet). Add the parsley, season to taste and toss together. Continue to cook for 1–2 minutes to heat through. Pile on to warmed serving plates, spooning over the cooking juices.

VARIATIONS

Most varieties of pasta work well in this recipe, and strands look particularly attractive.

Wholemeal (wholewheat) pasta doesn't have any egg added to the dough, so it is low in fat, and higher in fibre than other pastas.

Prawns (shrimp) or chopped crab meat would make a suitable alternative to either mussels or scallops, and 350 g/12 oz/ 2 cups diced cooked chicken would give a good alternative for non-shellfish eaters.

FILLED SOLE & SMOKED SALMON ROLLS

In this elegant dish, which is ideal for special occasions, the delicate flavour of sole and salmon blend together perfectly with a light, citrus filling.

STEP 1

SERVES: 4

PREPARATION: 20 MINS,
    COOKING 17 MINS

CALS/KJ PER PORTION: 170/715
FAT PER PORTION: 4 G

60 g/2 oz/1 cup fresh wholemeal (whole wheat) breadcrumbs
½ tsp grated lime rind
1 tbsp lime juice
60 g/2 oz/¼ cup low-fat soft cheese
4 × 125 g/4 oz sole fillets
60 g/2 oz smoked salmon
150 ml/¼ pint/⅔ cup Fresh Fish Stock (see page 78)
150 ml/¼ pint/⅔ cup low-fat natural yogurt
1 tbsp chopped fresh chervil
salt and pepper
fresh chervil to garnish

TO SERVE:
selection of freshly steamed vegetables
lime wedges

1 In a mixing bowl, combine the breadcrumbs, lime rind and juice, soft cheese and seasoning, to form a soft stuffing mixture.

2 Skin the sole fillets by inserting a sharp knife in between the skin and flesh at the tail end. Holding the skin in your fingers and keeping it taut, strip the flesh away from the skin.

3 Halve the sole fillets lengthwise. Place strips of smoked salmon over the skinned side of each fillet, trimming the salmon as necessary.

4 Spoon one-eighth of the stuffing on to each fish fillet and press down along the fish with the back of a spoon. Carefully roll up from the head to the tail end. Place, seam-side down, in an ovenproof dish and pour in the stock. Bake in a preheated oven at 190°C/375°F/Gas Mark 5 for 15 minutes.

5 Using a fish slice, transfer the fish to a warm serving plate, cover and keep warm. Pour the cooking juices into a saucepan and add the yogurt and chopped chervil. Season to taste and heat gently without boiling. Garnish the fish rolls with chervil and serve with the yogurt sauce, and the steamed vegetables and lime wedges.

STEP 2

STEP 3

STEP 4

STEP 1

STEP 2

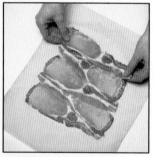

STEP 3

STEP 4

ORIENTAL MONKFISH TAIL WITH SWEET & SOUR VEGETABLES

Use a two-layered steamer for this recipe so you can cook the fish in one layer and the vegetables in the other.

SERVES: 6
PREPARATION: 40 MINS,
  COOKING: 40 MINS

CALS/KJ PER PORTION: 277/1162
FAT PER PORTION: 14.2 G

*750 g/1½ lb monkfish tail
175 g/6 oz peeled prawns (shrimp),
  defrosted if frozen
4 spring onions (scallions), chopped
1 fresh red chilli, seeded and finely chopped
2 tbsp oyster sauce
175 g/6 oz/6 slices lean rindless back bacon*

SWEET & SOUR VEGETABLES:
*250 g/8 oz/2 courgettes (zucchini), trimmed
250 g/8 oz/2–3 carrots, peeled
1 red (bell) pepper, deseeded
125 g/4 oz/1⅓ cups mangetout (snow peas),
  prepared
½ tsp grated lemon rind*

SAUCE:
*300 ml/½ pint/1¼ cups Fresh Fish Stock
  (see page 78)
4 tbsp white wine vinegar
1 tbsp caster (superfine) sugar
2 tbsp tomato purée (paste)
2 tbsp light soy sauce
2 tsp cornflour (cornstarch) mixed with
  4 tsp cold water*

1 Strip away the skin and membrane from the monkfish. Slice in half by cutting along the sides of the central bone.

2 Lay the fish between 2 layers of baking parchment and flatten to 1 cm/½ inch thick with a rolling pin. Mix the remaining ingredients, except the bacon, to form a stuffing.

3 Press stuffing on to one half of the fish and top with the other piece. Lay 5 slices of bacon on baking parchment and place the fish on top. Fold the bacon over the fish and cover with the remaining bacon slice. Secure with string. Place the fish into 1 compartment of a large steamer. Bring a wok of water to the boil and put the steamer on top. Cover and steam for 20 minutes.

4 Meanwhile slice the vegetables except the mangetout. Place in the second steaming compartment with the mangetout and lemon rind. Turn the fish over and place the vegetable compartment on top. Steam for 10 minutes until cooked.

5 To make sauce, put the ingredients into a pan. Bring to the boil, stirring, and simmer for 5 minutes. Slice fish and serve with vegetables and sauce.

STEP 1

STEP 2

STEP 3

STEP 4

GRILLED PLAICE WITH MIXED MUSHROOMS

Gentle grilling (broiling) ensures the moist texture of fish is retained during cooking, and in this recipe the plaice is complemented by the texture of mushrooms.

SERVES: 4
PREPARATION: 15 MINS,
COOKING: 16 MINS

CALS/KJ PER PORTION: 210/884
FAT PER PORTION: 11.2 G

*4 × 150 g/ 5 oz white-skinned plaice fillets
2 tbsp lime juice
90 g/ 3 oz/¹/₃ cup low-fat spread
300 g/ 10 oz/ 2¹/₂ cups mixed small
   mushrooms such as button, oyster,
   shiitake, chanterelle or morel, sliced or
   quartered
4 tomatoes, skinned (see page 18), seeded
   and chopped
celery salt and pepper
basil leaves to garnish
mixed salad to serve*

1 Line a grill (broiler) rack with baking parchment and place the fish on top.

2 Sprinkle over the lime juice and season with celery salt and pepper. Place under a preheated moderate grill (broiler) and cook for 7–8 minutes without turning, until just cooked. Keep warm.

3 Meanwhile, gently melt the low fat spread in a non-stick frying pan (skillet), add the mushrooms and fry for 4–5 minutes over a low heat until cooked.

4 Gently heat the tomatoes in a small saucepan. Spoon the mushrooms, with any pan juices, and the tomatoes over the plaice.

5 Garnish with basil leaves and serve with a light salad.

MUSHROOMS

There are many varieties of mushrooms available now from greengrocers and supermarkets. Experiment with different mushrooms; they are ideal in a low-fat diet, as they are packed full of flavour and contain no fat. More 'meaty' types of mushroom like chestnut (crimini), will take slightly longer to cook.

CHAPTER THREE

Meat Dishes

The healthy diet promoted by the majority of supermarkets and shops has meant that leaner, lower-fat cuts of meat and poultry are now available. They are usually more expensive because of the higher quality and the longer preparation time, so buy less and serve with lots of tasty vegetables or low-fat sauces: you will not end up spending more and you'll be the healthier for it!

Chicken and turkey are lower in fat than lamb, pork and beef; liver, kidney, venison and rabbit are also relatively low in fat. Look out for the extra lean minced (ground) meats now available. They can still be dry-fried over a low heat without the addition of oil or fat.

The addition of fruit in several of the following recipes helps with the digestion and makes for some interesting meals.

Opposite: *Lean and tender cuts of meat combine with tasty sauces to create delicious main meals.*

STEP 1

STEP 2

STEP 3

STEP 4

CHICKEN & MANGO TIKKA KEBABS

Chicken tikka is one of the lower-fat Indian dishes. Recipes vary but you can try your own combination of spices to suit your personal taste.

SERVES: 4
PREPARATION: 2 HRS 19 MINS,
  COOKING: 19 MINS

CALS/KJ PER PORTION: 204/858
FAT PER PORTION: 5.1 G

*4 × 125 g/4 oz boneless, skinless chicken
  breasts, cut into 2.5 cm/1 inch cubes
1 garlic clove, crushed
1 tsp grated ginger root
1 fresh green chilli, seeded and chopped
  finely
6 tbsp low-fat natural yogurt
1 tbsp tomato purée (paste)
1 tsp ground cumin
1 tsp ground coriander
1 tsp ground turmeric
1 large ripe mango
1 tbsp lime juice
salt and pepper
fresh coriander (cilantro) leaves to garnish*

*TO SERVE:
boiled white rice
lime wedges
mixed salad
warmed naan bread*

1 Cube the chicken and place in a shallow dish.

2 Mix together the garlic, ginger, chilli, yogurt, tomato purée (paste), cumin, ground coriander, turmeric and seasoning. Spoon over the chicken, mix well, cover and chill for 2 hours.

3 Using a vegetable peeler, peel the skin from the mango. Slice down either side of the stone (pit) and cut the mango flesh into cubes. Toss in lime juice, cover and chill until required.

4 Thread the chicken and mango pieces alternately on 8 skewers. Place the skewers on a grill (broiler) rack and brush the chicken with the yogurt marinade and the lime juice left from the mango.

5 Place under a preheated moderate grill (broiler) for 6–7 minutes. Turn over, brush again with the yogurt marinade and lime juice and cook for a further 6–7 minutes until the chicken juices run clear when the cubes are pierced with a sharp knife.

6 Serve on a bed of rice on a warmed platter, garnished with fresh coriander (cilantro) leaves and accompanied by lime wedges, a mixed salad and warmed naan bread.

STEP 1

STEP 2

STEP 3

STEP 4

CHICKEN WITH VERMOUTH, GRAPES & ARTICHOKES

The aromatic flavour of vermouth makes a good base for a sauce, and when partnered with refreshing grapes, ensures a delicious meal.

SERVES: 4
PREPARATION: 10 MINS,
　COOKING 45 MINS

CALS/KJ PER PORTION: 217/912
FAT PER PORTION: 4.7 G

*4 × 175 g/6 oz 'part-boned' chicken breasts,
　skinned
150 ml/¹/₄ pint/²/₃ cup dry white vermouth
150 ml/¹/₄ pint/²/₃ cup Fresh Chicken Stock
　(see page 76)
2 shallots, sliced thinly
about 400 g/13 oz can artichoke hearts,
　drained and halved
125 g/4 oz/³/₄ cup seedless green grapes
1 tbsp cornflour (cornstarch) mixed with
　2 tbsp cold water
salt and pepper
watercress sprigs to garnish
freshly cooked vegetables to serve*

1 Cook the chicken in a heavy-based non-stick frying pan (skillet) for 2–3 minutes on each side until sealed. Drain on paper towels.

2 Rinse out the pan, then add the dry vermouth and stock. Bring to the boil and add the shallots and chicken. Cover and simmer for 35 minutes.

3 Season to taste. Stir in the artichokes and grapes and heat through for 2–3 minutes.

4 Stir in the cornflour (cornstarch) mixture until thickened. Garnish with watercress sprigs and serve with freshly cooked vegetables.

PART-BONED CHICKEN BREASTS

Part-boned chicken breasts are very suitable for pan-cooking and casseroling, as they stay moist and tender. Try using chicken quarters if part-boned breasts are unavailable.

VERMOUTH

Vermouth is a mixture of wines. It is fortified, and enriched with a secret blend of herbs and spices. It is available in sweet and dry forms. Dry white wine would make a suitable substitute in this recipe.

CRANBERRY TURKEY BURGERS WITH SAGE & ONION

This recipe is bound to be popular with children and is easy to prepare for their supper or tea.

STEP 1

SERVES: 4
PREPARATION: 45 MINS,
  COOKING: 25 MINS

CALS/KJ PER PORTION: 193/810
FAT PER PORTION: 2.9 G

350 g/12 oz/1½ cups lean minced (ground) turkey
1 onion, chopped finely
1 tbsp chopped fresh sage
6 tbsp dry white breadcrumbs
4 tbsp cranberry sauce
1 egg white, size 2, lightly beaten
2 tsp sunflower oil
salt and pepper

TO SERVE:
4 toasted granary or wholemeal (whole wheat) burger buns
½ iceberg lettuce, shredded
4 tomatoes, sliced
4 tsp cranberry sauce

1 Mix together the turkey, onion, sage, seasoning, breadcrumbs and cranberry sauce, then bind with egg white. The mixture needs to be quite soft to prevent drying out during cooking.

2 Divide the mixture into 4 and press into 10 cm/4 inch rounds, about 2 cm/¾ inch thick; flour your hands with cornflour (cornstarch) if necessary. Line a plate with baking parchment, arrange the turkey burgers on top, cover and chill for 30 minutes.

STEP 2

3 Line a grill (broiler) rack with baking parchment, making sure the ends are secured underneath the rack to ensure they don't catch fire. Place the burgers on top and brush lightly with oil. Put under a preheated moderate grill (broiler) and cook for 10 minutes.

4 Carefully turn the burgers over, brush again with oil and cook for a further 12–15 minutes until cooked through. Drain on paper towels and keep warm.

STEP 3

5 Fill the burger rolls with lettuce, tomato and a burger, and top with cranberry sauce.

TIPS

Look out for a variety of ready minced (ground) meats at your butchers or supermarket. If unavailable, you can mince (grind) your own by choosing lean cuts and process them in a blender or food processor.

STEP 4

STEP 1

STEP 4

STEP 5

STEP 6

CANNELLONI

Traditionally a rich dish of meat, cheese and sauces, this lighter version is equally delicious and satisfying.

SERVES: 4
PREPARATION: 20 MINS,
   COOKING: 24 MINS

CALS/KJ PER PORTION: 344/1445
FAT PER PORTION: 12.5 G

150 g/ 5 oz/ 2¹/₂ cups button mushrooms
250 g/ 8 oz/ 1 cup lean minced (ground) beef
1 large red onion, chopped finely
1 garlic clove, crushed
¹/₂ tsp ground nutmeg
1 tsp dried mixed herbs
2 tbsp tomato purée (paste)
4 tbsp dry red wine
12 dried 'quick cook' cannelloni tubes
salt and pepper
mixed salad to serve

TOMATO SAUCE:
1 red onion, chopped finely
1 large carrot, grated
1 celery stick, chopped finely
1 dried bay leaf
150 ml/¹/₄ pint/²/₃ cup dry red wine
about 400 g/ 13 oz can chopped tomatoes
2 tbsp tomato purée (paste)
1 tsp caster (superfine) sugar
salt and pepper

TO GARNISH:
plum tomato
fresh basil sprig
30g/ 1oz Parmesan cheese shavings

1 Finely chop the mushrooms. In a non-stick frying pan (skillet), gently dry-fry the minced (ground) beef, onion, mushrooms and garlic for 3–4 minutes until browned all over.

2 Stir in the nutmeg, mixed herbs, seasoning, tomato purée (paste) and wine. Simmer gently for 15–20 minutes, until thick. Cool for 10 minutes.

3 To make the sauce, place the onion, carrot, celery, bay leaf and wine in a saucepan. Bring to the boil and simmer for 5 minutes until the liquid is reduced and the vegetables softened slightly.

4 Add the remaining ingredients and bring to the boil. Simmer for 15 minutes. Discard the bay leaf.

5 Spoon ¹/₄ of the sauce over the base of an ovenproof dish. Using a teaspoon, fill the cannelloni with the meat mixture and place on the sauce.

6 Spoon over the remaining sauce. Cover with foil and bake in a preheated oven at 200°C/400°F/Gas Mark 6 for 35–40 minutes until tender.

7 Garnish with the Parmesan cheese, plum tomato and basil sprig and serve with a mixed salad.

STEP 1

STEP 2

STEP 3

STEP 4

PORK WITH BLACKBERRIES & APPLE

We are accustomed to certain meat/fruit combinations, but this unusual one really is a delicious dish of tender cooked meat with luscious juicy fruits.

SERVES: 4
PREPARATION: 15 MINS,
  COOKING: 20 MINS

CALS/KJ PER PORTION: 267/1123
FAT PER PORTION: 9.8 G

500 g/1 lb piece lean pork fillet (tenderloin)
2 tsp sunflower oil
150 ml/¼ pint/⅔ cup Fresh Vegetable
  Stock (see page 77)
150 ml/¼ pint/⅔ cup dry rosé wine
1 tbsp chopped fresh thyme
1 tbsp clear honey
2 green-skinned dessert apples, cored and
  sliced, and tossed in 1 tbsp lemon juice
175 g/6 oz/1¼ cups prepared fresh or
  frozen blackberries, or 213 g/7½ oz can
  blackberries in natural juice, drained
2 tsp cornflour (cornstarch) mixed with
  4 tsp cold water
salt and pepper
freshly cooked vegetables to serve

1 Trim away any fat and silvery skin from the pork fillet and cut into 1 cm/½ inch thick slices, taking care to keep the slices a good shape.

2 Heat the oil in a non-stick frying pan (skillet), add the pork slices and fry for 4–5 minutes until browned all over. Using a perforated spoon, transfer the pork to paper towels; reserve the pan juices.

3 Pour the stock and wine into the pan with the juices and add the thyme and honey. Mix well, bring to a simmer and add the pork and apples. Continue to simmer, uncovered, for 5 minutes.

4 Add the blackberries, season to taste and simmer for a further 5 minutes. Stir in the cornflour (cornstarch) mixture until thickened. Serve with freshly cooked vegetables.

BLACKBERRIES

This dish works very well with fresh blackberries, but the type that are frozen or canned in natural juice make a suitable substitute.

VARIATION

You can also make this recipe with raspberries or even blueberries.

STEP 1

STEP 2

STEP 3

STEP 4

ROSEMARY & REDCURRANT LAMB FILLET (TENDERLOIN) WITH LEEK & POTATO MASH

This is a pretty dish of pink tender lamb served on a light green bed of mashed leeks and potatoes.

SERVES: 4
PREPARATION: 20 MINS,
  COOKING: 53 MINS

CALS/KJ PER PORTION: 340/1427
FAT PER PORTION: 10.4 G

500 g/1 lb lean lamb fillet (tenderloin)
4 tbsp redcurrant jelly
1 tbsp chopped fresh rosemary
1 garlic clove, crushed
500 g/1 lb potatoes, diced
500 g/1 lb leeks, sliced
150 ml/¹/₄ pint/²/₃ cup Fresh Vegetable
  Stock, (see page 77)
4 tsp low-fat natural fromage frais
salt and pepper
freshly steamed vegetables to serve

TO GARNISH:
chopped fresh rosemary
redcurrants

1 Put the lamb in a shallow baking tin (pan). Blend 2 tablespoons of the redcurrant jelly with the rosemary, garlic and seasoning. Brush over the lamb and cook in a preheated oven at 230°C/450°F/Gas Mark 8, brushing occasionally with any cooking juices, for 30 minutes.

2 Meanwhile, place the potatoes in a saucepan and cover with water. Bring to the boil, and cook for 8 minutes until softened. Drain well. Put the leeks in a saucepan with the stock. Cover and simmer for 7–8 minutes or until soft. Drain, reserving the cooking liquid.

3 Place the potato and leeks in a bowl and mash with a potato masher. Season to taste and stir in the fromage frais. Pile on to a warmed platter and keep warm.

4 In a saucepan, melt the remaining redcurrant jelly and stir in the leek cooking liquid. Bring to the boil for 5 minutes.

5 Slice the lamb and arrange over the mash. Spoon the sauce over the top. Garnish with rosemary and redcurrants and serve with freshly steamed vegetables.

CHAPTER FOUR

Vegetables & Salads

It is often easy to forget that accompaniments can pile on the calories and increase the fat content of a meal. It is not necessarily the vegetables or cereals that contain the fat but the dressings and sauces in which they are cooked or served. So with some care taken in preparation and cooking, you can still have your fill of vegetables and salads.

Vegetables and salads are ideal hunger-pang beaters. They are packed full of fibre and texture, so require a lot of chewing, and if you eat more slowly, you will feel satisfyingly full, without having consumed lots of fat.

In this chapter there's a sumptuous selection of hot and cold vegetables and salads for you to choose from, some mixing sweet and savoury, others containing spices and rich flavours from other countries, and some giving a different twist to traditional and much-loved vegetables.

Opposite: A wide selection of vegetables available at supermarkets ensures that vegetable meals will never be boring.

CHICK-PEA (GARBANZO BEAN), TOMATO & AUBERGINE (EGGPLANT) SALAD

A tasty Middle Eastern-style accompaniment, perfect to serve with lamb or chicken dishes.

STEP 1

STEP 2

STEP 4

STEP 5

SERVES: 4
PREPARATION: 1 HR 45 MINS,
    COOKING: 23 MINS

CALS/KJ PER PORTION: 231/971
FAT PER PORTION: 6.2 G

500 g/1 lb aubergines (eggplant)
4 tbsp salt
1 tbsp olive oil
1 large onion, chopped
1 garlic clove, crushed
150 ml/¼ pint/⅔ cup Fresh Vegetable
    Stock (see page 77)
about 400 g/13 oz can chopped tomatoes
2 tbsp tomato purée (paste)
1 tsp ground cinnamon
2 tsp caster (superfine) sugar
1 tbsp chopped fresh coriander (cilantro)
1 tbsp lemon juice
about 425 g/14 oz can chick-peas (garbanzo
    beans), drained
freshly ground black pepper
fresh coriander (cilantro) sprigs to garnish

TO SERVE:
warmed pitta (pocket) bread
lemon wedges

1 Cut the aubergines (eggplant) into 1 cm/½ inch thick slices and then cube. Layer in a bowl, sprinkling well with salt as you go. Set aside for 30 minutes for the bitter juices to drain out.

2 Transfer to a colander and rinse well under running cold water to remove the salt. Drain well and pat dry with paper towels.

3 Heat the oil in a large non-stick frying pan (skillet), add the onion and garlic and fry gently for 2–3 minutes until slightly softened.

4 Pour in the stock and bring to the boil. Add the aubergines (eggplant), canned tomatoes, tomato purée (paste), cinnamon, sugar and pepper. Mix well and simmer gently, uncovered, for 20 minutes until softened. Set aside to cool completely.

5 Stir in the fresh coriander (cilantro), lemon juice and chick-peas (garbanzo beans), cover and chill for 1 hour.

6 Garnish with coriander (cilantro) sprigs and serve with warmed pitta (pocket) bread and lemon wedges.

STEP 1

STEP 2

STEP 3

STEP 4

CARROT, CELERIAC (CELERY ROOT), CELERY & ORANGE SALAD

A crunchy and colourful, sweet and savoury dish which would also make an excellent appetizer.

SERVES: **6**
PREPARATION: **15** MINS

CALS/KJ PER PORTION: **126/529**
FAT PER PORTION: **5.5** G

500 g/1 lb celeriac (celery root)
2 tbsp orange juice
350 g/12 oz/4 carrots, sliced finely
2 celery sticks, chopped finely
30 g/1 oz/1 cup celery leaves
4 oranges
30 g/1 oz/¼ cup walnut pieces

DRESSING:
1 tbsp walnut oil
½ tsp grated orange rind
3 tbsp orange juice
1 tbsp white wine vinegar
1 tsp clear honey
salt and pepper

1 Trim and peel the celeriac (celery root) and slice or grate finely into a bowl. Add the orange juice and toss together.

2 Mix in the carrots, celery and celery leaves. Cover and chill while preparing the oranges.

3 Slice off the tops and bottoms from the oranges. Using a sharp knife, slice off the skin, taking the pith away at the same time. Cut out the orange flesh by slicing along the side of the membranes dividing the segments. Gently mix the segments into the celeriac (celery root) mixture.

4 To make the dressing, place all the ingredients in a small screw-top jar. Seal and shake well to mix.

5 Pile the vegetable mixture on to a plate. Sprinkle over the walnut pieces and serve with the dressing.

CELERIAC (CELERY ROOT)

Celeriac (celery root) is a variety of celery with a bulbous, knobbly root. It has a rough, light brown skin and creamy white flesh. It is delicious raw or cooked. In this salad, it combines well with carrots and celery for a vitamin- and fibre-rich dish.

STEP 1

STEP 2

STEP 3

STEP 3

HOT & SPICY GOLDEN RICE SALAD

Serve this Indian-style dish with a low-fat natural yogurt salad for a refreshing contrast.

SERVES: 4
PREPARATION: 30 MINS,
   COOKING: 18 MINS

CALS/KJ PER PORTION: 499/2094
FAT PER PORTION: 7 G

2 tsp vegetable oil
1 onion, chopped finely
1 fresh red chilli, deseeded and chopped finely
8 cardamom pods
1 tsp ground turmeric
1 tsp garam masala
350 g/12 oz 1³/₄ cups basmati rice, rinsed
700 ml/1¹/₄ pints 3 cups boiling water
1 orange bell pepper, chopped
250 g/8 oz cauliflower florets, divided into small sprigs
4 ripe tomatoes, skinned, deseeded, and chopped (see page 18)
125 g/4 oz/³/₄ cup seedless raisins
30 g/1 oz/¹/₄ cup toasted flaked (slivered) almonds
salt and pepper
salad of low-fat natural yogurt, onion, cucumber and mint to serve

1 Heat the oil in a large non-stick saucepan, add the onion, chilli, cardamom pods, turmeric and garam masala and fry gently for 2–3 minutes until the vegetables are just softened.

2 Stir in the rice, boiling water, seasoning, (bell) pepper and cauliflower. Cover with a tight-fitting lid, bring to the boil, then cook over a low heat for 15 minutes without lifting the lid.

3 Uncover, fork through and stir in the tomatoes and raisins. Cover again, turn off the heat and leave for 15 minutes. Discard the cardamom pods.

4 Pile on to a warmed serving platter and sprinkle over the toasted flaked (slivered) almonds. Serve with the yogurt salad.

BASMATI RICE

Indian basmati rice is more expensive than long-grain, but it has a fragrant flavour and fluffy texture. Rinse or soak it before cooking to remove the excess starch.

ORIENTAL VEGETABLE NOODLES

This dish has a mild, nutty flavour from the peanut butter and dry-roasted peanuts.

STEP 1

SERVES: 4
PREPARATION: 10 MINS,
    COOKING: 7 MINS

CALS/KJ PER PORTION: 279/1171
FAT PER PORTION: 7.6 G

*175 g/6 oz/1½ cups green thread noodles
    or multi-coloured spaghetti*
1 tsp sesame oil
2 tbsp crunchy peanut butter
2 tbsp light soy sauce
1 tbsp white wine vinegar
1 tsp clear honey
125 g/4 oz daikon (mooli), grated
125 g/4 oz/1 large carrot, grated
125 g/4 oz cucumber, shredded finely
*1 bunch spring onions (scallions), shredded
    finely*
1 tbsp dry-roasted peanuts, crushed

TO GARNISH:
carrot flowers
spring onion (scallion) tassels

 Bring a large saucepan of water to the boil, add the noodles or spaghetti and cook according to the packet instructions. Drain well and rinse in cold water. Leave in a bowl of cold water until required.

2 Put the sesame oil, peanut butter, soy sauce, vinegar, honey and seasoning into a small screw-top jar. Seal and shake well to mix.

3 Drain the noodles or spaghetti well, place in a large serving bowl and mix in half the peanut sauce.

4 Using 2 forks, toss in the daikon (mooli), carrot, cucumber and spring onions (scallions). Sprinkle with crushed peanuts and garnish with carrot flowers and spring onion (scallion) tassels. Serve with the remaining peanut sauce.

NOODLES

There are many varieties of oriental noodles available from oriental markets, delicatessens and supermarkets. Try rice noodles, which contain very little fat and require little cooking; usually soaking in boiling water is sufficient.

STEP 2

STEP 3

STEP 4

STEP 1

STEP 2

STEP 3

STEP 4

STEAMED VEGETABLES WITH HOT TAHINI & GARLIC DIP

Fresh vegetables are full of flavour and texture when steamed and this tasty dip makes a perfect accompaniment.

SERVES: 4
PREPARATION: 10 MINS,
  COOKING: 15 MINS

CALS/KJ PER PORTION: 142/595
FAT PER PORTION: 6.9 G

250 g/8 oz small broccoli florets
250 g/8 oz small cauliflower florets
250 g/8 oz asparagus, sliced into 5 cm/2
  inch lengths
2 small red onions, quartered
1 tbsp lime juice
2 tsp toasted sesame seeds
1 tbsp chopped fresh chives to garnish

HOT TAHINI & GARLIC DIP:
1 tsp sunflower oil
2 garlic cloves, crushed
1/2–1 tsp chilli powder
2 tsp tahini paste
150 ml/1/4 pint/2/3 cup low-fat natural
  fromage frais
2 tbsp chopped fresh chives
salt and pepper

1 Line the base of a steamer with baking parchment and arrange the vegetables on top. Bring a wok or large saucepan of water to the boil, and place the steamer on top. Sprinkle with lime juice and steam for 10 minutes.

2 To make the dip, heat the oil in a small non-stick saucepan, add the garlic, chilli powder and seasoning and fry gently for 2–3 minutes until the garlic is softened.

3 Remove from the heat and stir in the tahini paste and fromage frais. Return to the heat and cook gently for 1–2 minutes without boiling. Stir in the chives.

4 Remove the vegetables from the steamer and place on a warmed serving platter. Sprinkle with the sesame seeds and garnish with chopped chives. Serve with the hot dip.

TAHINI

Tahini is an oily paste made from roasted sesame seeds. It is a staple ingredient in the cooking of countries around the eastern end of the Mediterranean. It has a strong, nutty flavour and a high fat content, but a little goes a long way, so use sparingly to keep the fat content down.

STEP 1

STEP 2

STEP 3

STEP 4

LAYERED ROOT VEGETABLE GRATIN

The word 'gratin' usually describes a baked crust made from eggs and flour. In this recipe an assortment of vegetables are cooked in a light nutmeg sauce with a potato and cheese topping.

SERVES: 6
PREPARATION: 20 MINS,
  COOKING: 1 HR 19 MINS

CALS/KJ PER PORTION: 218/916
FAT PER PORTION: 9 G

250 g/8 oz/2 large carrots
250 g/8 oz baby parsnips
1 fennel bulb
500 g/1 lb/3 potatoes
90 g/3 oz/^{1}/$_3$ cup low-fat spread
30 g/1 oz/^{1}/$_4$ cup plain (all-purpose) flour
300 ml/^{1}/$_2$ pint/1^1/$_4$ cups skimmed milk
^{1}/$_2$ tsp ground nutmeg
1 egg, beaten
30 g/1 oz/^{1}/$_4$ cup freshly grated Parmesan
  cheese
salt and pepper

TO SERVE:
crusty bread
tomatoes

1 Cut the carrots and parsnips into thin lengthwise strips. Cook in boiling water for 5 minutes. Drain well and transfer to an ovenproof baking dish.

2 Thinly slice the fennel and cook in boiling water for 2–3 minutes.

Drain well and add to the carrots and parsnips. Season.

3 Peel and dice the potatoes into 2 cm/^{3}/$_4$ inch cubes. Cook in boiling water for 6 minutes. Drain well and set aside.

4 Gently melt half the low-fat spread and stir in the flour. Remove from the heat and gradually mix in the milk. Return to the heat and stir until thickened. Season and stir in the nutmeg. Cool for 10 minutes.

5 Beat in the egg and spoon over the vegetables. Arrange the potatoes on top and sprinkle over the cheese. Dot with the remaining low-fat spread. Bake in a preheated oven at 180°C/350°F/Gas Mark 4 for 1 hour until the vegetables are tender.

6 Serve as a light meal with crusty bread and a salad, or as an accompaniment to a light main course, such as steamed fish or grilled chicken.

CHAPTER FIVE

Puddings & Desserts

Just because you're watching the fat content in your diet doesn't mean you have to miss out on a pudding! This is a notorious area of the diet for piling on the calories and indulging in cream-laden, buttery dishes. But with a few easy and tasty alternatives you can still enjoy a sweet treat without the bulging waist-line and that distended feeling at the end of a meal.

Fruit is an excellent base for a dessert and we have so much to choose from, thanks to world trade. You're bound to find something you like whatever the time of year; and the best thing about fruit is that most of it contains no fat at all and it is rich in natural sugar, vitamins and fibre – perfect for the low-fat diet!

Opposite: *The varied selection of fruit now on sale means those watching their weight can still enjoy rich sweet desserts without worrying about the calories.*

STEP 1

STEP 2

STEP 3

STEP 4

SUMMER FRUIT BATTER PUDDING

Serve this mouth-watering French-style pudding hot or cold with low-fat fromage frais or yogurt.

SERVES: 6
PREPARATION: 1 HR 40 MINS,
COOKING: 50 MINS

CALS/KJ PER PORTION: 204/857
FAT PER PORTION: 2.5 G

*500 g/1 lb prepared fresh assorted soft
  fruits such as blackberries, raspberries,
  strawberries, blueberries, cherries,
  gooseberries, redcurrants, blackcurrants
4 tbsp soft fruit liqueur such as crème de
  cassis, kirsch or framboise
4 tbsp skimmed milk powder
125 g/4 oz/1 cup plain (all-purpose) flour
pinch of salt
60 g/2 oz/¹/₄ cup caster (superfine) sugar
2 eggs, size 2, beaten
300 ml/¹/₂ pint/1¹/₄ cups skimmed milk
1 tsp vanilla flavouring (extract)
2 tsp caster (superfine) sugar to dust*

*TO SERVE:
assorted soft fruits
low-fat yogurt or natural fromage frais*

1 Place the assorted fruits in a mixing bowl and spoon over the fruit liqueur. Cover and chill for 1 hour for the fruit to macerate.

2 In a large bowl, mix the skimmed milk powder, flour, salt and sugar.

Make a well in the centre and gradually whisk in the eggs, milk and vanilla flavouring (extract), using a balloon whisk, until smooth. Transfer to a jug, and set aside for 30 minutes.

3 Line the base of a 23 cm/9 inch round ovenproof baking dish with baking parchment and spoon in the fruits and juices.

4 Re-whisk the batter and pour over the fruits, stand the dish on a baking sheet and bake in a preheated oven at 200°C/400°F/Gas Mark 6 for 45–50 minutes until firm, risen and golden brown.

5 Dust with caster (superfine) sugar. Serve immediately from the baking dish, accompanied by extra fruits, low-fat natural yogurt or fromage frais.

VARIATIONS

This recipe is based on the French dessert called 'clafoutis', which is a rich batter filled with pitted cherries and kirsch. When in season, fresh cherries would make a delicious substitute in this recipe.

STEP 1

STEP 2

STEP 3

STEP 5

CINNAMON PEARS WITH MAPLE & RICOTTA CREAM

These spicy sweet pears are accompanied by a delicious melt-in-the-mouth cream; you won't believe it's low in fat!

SERVES: 4
PREPARATION: 10 MINS,
   COOKING: 22 MINS

CALS/KJ PER PORTION: 184/773
FAT PER PORTION: 5.7 G

1 lemon
4 firm ripe pears
300 ml/¹/₂ pint/ 1¹/₄ cups dry cider or
   unsweetened apple juice
1 cinnamon stick, broken in half
mint leaves to decorate

MAPLE RICOTTA CREAM:
125 g/4 oz/¹/₂ cup medium-fat Ricotta
   cheese
125 g/4 oz/¹/₂ cup low-fat natural fromage
   frais
¹/₂ tsp ground cinnamon
¹/₂ tsp grated lemon rind
1 tbsp maple syrup
lemon rind to decorate

1 Using a vegetable peeler, remove the rind from the lemon and place in a non-stick frying pan (skillet). Squeeze the lemon and pour into a shallow bowl.

2 Peel the pears, and halve and core them. Toss them in the lemon juice to prevent discolouration. Place in the frying pan (skillet) and pour over the remaining lemon juice.

3 Add the cider or apple juice and cinnamon stick halves. Gently bring to the boil, lower the heat so the liquid simmers and cook the pears for 10 minutes. Remove the pears using a perforated spoon; reserve the cooking juice. Put the pears in a warm heatproof serving dish, cover with foil and put in a warming drawer or low oven to keep warm.

4 Return the pan to the heat, bring to the boil, then simmer for 8–10 minutes until reduced by half. Spoon over the pears.

5 To make the maple Ricotta cream, mix together all the ingredients. Decorate with lemon rind and serve with the pears.

PEARS

Comice (Bartlett) or Conference pears are suitable for this recipe. Pears ripen quickly and can bruise easily. It's best to buy them a few days before you plan to cook them.

STEP 1

STEP 2

STEP 4

STEP 5

WINTER PUDDINGS

An interesting alternative to the familiar Summer Pudding that uses dried fruits and tasty malt loaf.

SERVES: 4
PREPARATION: **20 MINS, CHILLING: OVERNIGHT, COOKING: 10 MINS**

CALS/KJ PER PORTION: **353/1485**
FAT PER PORTION: **1.8** G

325 g/11 oz fruit malt loaf
150 g/5 oz/1 cup no-need-to-soak dried apricots, chopped coarsely
90 g/3 oz/¹/₂ cup dried apple, chopped coarsely
450 ml/³/₄ pint/2 cups orange juice
1 tsp grated orange rind
2 tbsp orange liqueur
grated orange rind to decorate
low-fat crème fraîche or low-fat natural fromage frais to serve

1 Cut the malt loaf into 5mm/¼ inch slices.

2 Place the apricots, apple and orange juice in a saucepan. Bring to the boil, then simmer for 10 minutes. Remove the fruit using a perforated spoon and reserve the liquid. Place the fruit in a shallow dish and leave to cool. Stir in the orange rind and liqueur.

3 Line 4 × 180 ml/6 fl oz/³/₄ cup pudding basins or ramekin dishes

with baking parchment. Cut 4 circles from the malt loaf slices to fit the tops of the moulds and cut the remaining slices to line the moulds.

4 Soak the malt loaf slices in the reserved fruit syrup, then arrange around the base and sides of the moulds. Trim away any crusts which overhang the edges. Fill the centres of the moulds with the chopped fruit, pressing down well, and place the malt loaf circles on top.

5 Cover with baking parchment and weigh each basin down with a 250 g/8 oz weight or a food can. Chill overnight.

6 Remove the weight and baking parchment. Carefully turn the puddings out on to 4 serving plates. Remove the lining paper. Decorate with grated orange rind and serve with low-fat crème fraîche or natural fromage frais.

STEP 2

STEP 3

STEP 4

STEP 6

ORANGE SYLLABUB WITH SPONGE HEARTS

A zesty, creamy whip made from yogurt and milk with a hint of orange, served with light and luscious sweet sponge cakes. You will need five oranges for this recipe.

SERVES: 4
PREPARATION: 1 HR 25 MINS,
 COOKING: 10 MINS

CALS/KJ PER PORTION: 398/1673
FAT PER PORTION: 3.9 G

4 oranges
600 ml/ 1 pint/ 2½ cups low-fat natural
 yogurt
6 tbsp low-fat skimmed milk powder
4 tbsp caster (superfine) sugar
1 tbsp grated orange rind
4 tbsp orange juice
2 egg whites
fresh orange zest to decorate

SPONGE HEARTS:
2 eggs, size 2
90 g/ 3 oz/ 6 tbsp caster (superfine) sugar
45 g/ 1½ oz/ 6 tbsp plain (all-purpose) flour
45 g/ 1½ oz/ 6 tbsp wholemeal (whole
 wheat) flour
1 tbsp hot water
1 tsp icing (confectioners') sugar

1 Slice off the tops and bottoms of the oranges and the skin. Then cut out the segments, removing the zest and membranes between each one. Divide the orange segments between 4 dessert glasses, then chill.

2 In a large mixing bowl, combine the yogurt, milk powder, sugar, orange rind and juice. Cover and chill for 1 hour until thickened.

3 Whisk the egg whites until stiff, then fold into the orange yogurt mixture. Pile on to the orange slices and chill for an hour. Decorate with fresh orange rind and sponge hearts.

4 To make the sponge hearts, line a 15 × 25 cm/6 × 10 inch baking tin (pan) with baking parchment. Whisk the eggs and caster (superfine) sugar until thick and pale. Sieve in the flours, then fold them in using a large metal spoon, adding the hot water at the same time.

5 Pour into the tin (pan) and bake in a preheated oven at 220°C/425°F/ Gas Mark 7 for 9–10 minutes until golden and firm to the touch.

6 Turn on to a sheet of baking parchment. Using a 5 cm/2 inch heart-shaped cutter, stamp out hearts. Transfer to a wire rack to cool. Lightly dust with icing (confectioners') sugar before serving with the syllabub.

STRAWBERRY ROSE BROWN SUGAR MERINGUES

The combination of aromatic strawberries and rose water with crisp caramelized sugar meringues makes this a truly irresistible dessert.

STEP 1

SERVES: 6
PREPARATION: 20 MINS,
  COOKING: 3 HRS 30 MINS

CALS/KJ PER PORTION: 146/612
FAT PER PORTION: 1 G

3 egg whites, size 2
pinch of salt
175 g/6 oz/1 cup light muscovado sugar,
  crushed to be free of lumps
250 g/8 oz/1½ cups strawberries, hulled
2 tsp rose water
150 ml/¼ pint/⅔ cup low-fat natural
  fromage frais
extra strawberries to serve (optional)

TO DECORATE:
rose-scented geranium leaves
rose petals

1 In a large grease-free bowl, whisk the egg whites and salt until very stiff and dry. Gradually whisk in the sugar a spoonful at a time, until the mixture is stiff again.

2 Line a baking sheet with baking parchment and drop 12 spoonfuls of the meringue mixture on to the sheet. Bake in a preheated oven at 120°C/250°F/Gas Mark ½ for 3–3½

hours, until completely dried out and crisp. Allow to cool.

3 Reserve 60 g/2 oz/⅓ cup of the strawberries. Place the remaining strawberries in a blender or food processor and blend for a few seconds until smooth. Alternatively, mash the strawberries with a fork and press through a sieve (strainer) to form a purée paste. Stir in the rose water. Chill until required.

4 To serve, slice the reserved strawberries. Sandwich the meringues together with fromage frais and sliced strawberries. Spoon the strawberry rose purée paste on to 6 serving plates and top with a meringue. Decorate with rose petals and rose-scented geranium leaves, and serve with extra strawberries if liked.

STEP 2

STEP 3

TIP

The brown sugar gives a treacley caramelized flavour. If preferred, you can use unbleached granulated sugar.

STEP 4

STEP 1

STEP 2

STEP 3

STEP 4

TROPICAL FRUIT RICE MOULD

A rice pudding with a twist. Light flakes of rice with a tang of pineapple and lime. You can serve it with any selection of your favourite fruits.

SERVES: 8
PREPARATION: 2 HRS 10 MINS,
COOKING: 20 MINS

CALS/KJ PER PORTION: 221/928
FAT PER PORTION: 1.4 G

250 g/8 oz/1 cup + 2 tbsp short-grain or
    pudding rice, rinsed
900 ml/1½ pints/3¾ cups skimmed milk
1 tbsp caster (superfine) sugar
4 tbsp white rum with coconut or
    unsweetened pineapple juice
180 ml/6 fl oz/¾ cup low-fat natural
    yogurt
about 425 g/14 oz can pineapple pieces in
    natural juice, drained and chopped
1 tsp grated lime rind
1 tbsp lime juice
1 sachet/1 envelope powdered gelatine
    dissolved in 3 tbsp boiling water
lime wedges to decorate
mixed tropical fruits such as passion-fruit,
    baby pineapple, paw-paw (papaya),
    mango, carambola (star fruit) to serve

1 Place the rice and milk in a saucepan. Bring to the boil, then simmer gently, uncovered, for 20 minutes until the rice is soft and the milk is absorbed. Stir the mixture occasionally and keep the heat low to prevent sticking. Transfer to a mixing bowl and leave to cool.

2 Stir the sugar, white rum with coconut or pineapple juice, yogurt, pineapple pieces, lime rind and juice into the rice. Fold into the gelatine mixture.

3 Rinse a 1.5 litre/2½ pint/1½ quart non-stick ring mould or ring cake tin (pan) with water and spoon in the rice mixture. Press down well and chill for 2 hours until firm.

4 To serve, loosen the rice from the mould with a small palette knife (spatula) and invert on to a serving plate. Decorate with lime wedges and fill the centre with assorted tropical fruits.

VARIATION

Try serving this dessert with a light sauce made from 300 ml/½ pint/1¼ cups tropical fruit or pineapple juice thickened with 2 tsp arrowroot.

LOW-FAT COOKING

HOMEMADE STOCK

Fresh Chicken Stock

MAKES: ABOUT 1.75 LITRES/
  3 PINTS/7½ CUPS
CALS/KJ PER 150 ML/¼ PINT/
  ⅔ CUP: 25/105
FAT PER 150 ML/¼ PINT/
  ⅔ CUP: LESS THAN 0.1 G

1 kg/2 lb chicken, skinned
2 celery sticks
1 onion
2 carrots
1 garlic clove
few sprigs of fresh parsley
2 litres/3½ pints/9 cups
  water
salt and pepper

1. Put all the ingredients into a large saucepan.

2. Bring to the boil. Skim away surface scum using a large flat spoon. Reduce the heat to a gentle simmer, partially cover, and cook for 2 hours. Allow to cool.

3. Line a sieve (strainer) with clean muslin (cheesecloth) and place over a large jug or bowl. Pour the stock through the sieve (strainer). The cooked chicken can be used in another recipe. Discard the other solids. Cover the stock and chill.

4. Skim away any fat that forms before using. Store in the refrigerator for 3–4 days, until required, or freeze in small batches.

CUTTTING DOWN ON FAT

Today we are all too familiar with the effects of too much fat in the diet. Affluent Western-style living has brought with it an increase in heart disease, obesity and cancer – all thought to be caused by the high fat intake in the modern diet. It is possible to enjoy a wide range of foods and have an interesting and satisfying diet yet keep our fat intake to moderate levels. You just need to adopt a few simple, common-sense, lifestyle changes for the better.

FOOD PREPARATION

Look out for lean cuts of meat and fish. Meat should be firm with pink or red flesh and as few streaks of fat as possible. Better quality meats will be more expensive, so buy less than normal and fill up with healthy low-fat vegetables instead. Fish should be fresh and clean with a low odour. Eyes should be bright, and flesh and skin should be firm and not too dry. Choose white flesh fish as opposed to darker oily varieties, as the latter are high in fat. Include these oily fish in the diet occasionally, unless otherwise advised, as they contain valuable nutrients in their oils. If you have a specific cholesterol problem, then avoid prawns (shrimp) as they have a relatively high cholesterol content. They can be eaten in moderation in a normal healthy diet, as they are low in fat.

Trim away as much visible fat as possible from meat and remove the skin of poultry before cooking, where applicable, and always before serving as the skin contains high levels of fat.

Once cooked, drain food on paper towels before serving to absorb any excess fat. Skim casseroles and soups with a flat ladle or blot with paper towels while cooking or upon cooling.

Avoid using ingredients with a high fat content like cream, butter and cooking oils. Try substituting with lower-fat foods like yogurt, fromage frais and low-fat spreads. There are so many varieties available to choose from it's worth taking a trip to the local supermarket to get some ideas for yourself. Most products have pack nutrition labelling so you can glance at the information and know instantly whether the product is suitable for your diet.

Don't let your food become boring and bland just because you're cutting down on the fat. Maximize flavours by adding spices and herbs to your cooking, and use interesting combinations of foods to tickle your tastebuds. Presentation is also important; making food look appetizing by adding attractive garnishes, or arranging the food on the plate in a decorative way, will enhance the appearance of a dish and often make smaller amounts of food look larger.

COOKING METHODS

Steaming is a very nutritious way of cooking, as it involves no addition of fat. Foods remain bright in colour, firm in texture and high in nutrition. You can use a stainless steel steamer or even a large sieve (strainer) with a lid placed over a large saucepan of boiling water.

Foods for grilling (broiling) or barbecuing will benefit from marinating prior to cooking. This will add flavour and moisture to the food as it cooks under the strong, radiant heat. Little or no oil will be needed to brush over the food providing the mixture is moist enough to prevent it from drying out. This is an excellent way of cooking foods, especially meat, as fat will drain away naturally during the cooking. If you are worried about turning food over in case it sticks to the grill (broiler) rack, then line the rack carefully with baking parchment. Make sure the ends of the parchment are tucked underneath to prevent them burning. Don't forget to drain the food on paper towels before serving.

Pan-cooking and stir-frying only use a minimum amount of cooking oil or fat to start the foods cooking and increase the flavour. After the initial gentle frying, liquid is added and then the food cooks in the moisture and steam, sealing in all the flavour and nutrients. Make sure the oil is hot enough at the start so that the food is sealed in the fat. If it is not hot, then the food will absorb it like a sponge.

Oven cooking or roasting traditionally involves the addition of fat. When cooking tender, leaner cuts of meat or poultry without oil, it is important to brush them with a sauce or liquid before and during cooking to prevent them from drying out.

COOKING EQUIPMENT
Non-stick pans and cookware are a good investment when on a low-fat diet, as they dramatically cut down the amount of oil necessary for cooking. They will also make life easier at the sink when it comes to the washing up! Heavier pans are preferable, as these will conduct the heat better and give more even cooking. Remember to use wooden or plastic implements in these pans, as metal will scratch the coating. Also look out for non-stick pan scourers as opposed to the traditional metal ones.

Baking parchment and paper towels are also important cooking aids. Baking parchment can be used in conventional, combination or microwave ovens, and it allows food to be turned out freely from tins (pans) and trays. Use it to line tins (pans) and dishes to prevent sticking; there is no need to grease. It can also be used to line grill (broiler) racks providing the flame is not too hot: otherwise it will ignite.

Absorbent kitchen paper is necessary for draining foods of any excess fat or oil they may retain. Look for plain paper, free from colour, to prevent transfer of dye to the food.

LOW-FAT FOODS
Cheese
There is a wide variety of different cheeses on the market for the low-fat diet. Traditional cheeses like Cheddar and Stilton (blue cheese) have a relatively high fat content. Look for reduced-fat Cheddar-type cheeses as a substitute.

Cottage cheese is a fresh curd cheese which is naturally low in fat, but for a further fat reduction look out for low-fat cottage cheese.

Fresh Vegetable Stock

MAKES: ABOUT 1.5 LITRES/
2$\frac{1}{2}$ PINTS/6$\frac{1}{4}$ CUPS
CALS/KJ PER 150 ML/
$\frac{1}{4}$ PINTS/$\frac{2}{3}$ CUP: 19/80
FAT PER 150 ML/$\frac{1}{4}$ PINT/
$\frac{2}{3}$ CUP: TRACE

1 large onion, sliced
1 large carrot, diced
1 stick celery, chopped
2 garlic cloves
1 dried bay leaf
few sprigs of fresh parsley
pinch of grated nutmeg
2 litres/3$\frac{1}{2}$ pints/9 cups
    water
salt and pepper

1. Place all the ingredients in a large saucepan and bring to the boil.

2. Skim off surface scum using a flat spoon. Reduce the heat to a gentle simmer, partially cover, and cook for 45 minutes. Leave to cool.

3. Line a sieve (strainer) with clean muslin (cheesecloth) and place over a large jug or bowl. Pour the stock through the sieve (strainer). Discard the solids. Cover the stock and store in the refrigerator for up to 3 days until required, or freeze in small batches.

Fresh Fish Stock

MAKES: ABOUT 1.75 LITRES/
3 PINTS/7½ CUPS
CALS/KJ PER 150 ML/¼ PINT/
⅔ CUP:15/63
FAT PER 150 ML/¼ PINT/
⅔ CUP: LESS THAN 0.1G

1 kg/2 lb white fish bones,
  heads and scraps
1 large onion, chopped
2 carrots, chopped
2 celery sticks, chopped
½ tsp black peppercorns
½ tsp grated lemon rind
few sprigs of fresh parsley
2 litres/3½ pints/9 cups
  water
salt and pepper

1. Rinse the fish trimmings well in cold water and place in a large saucepan with the other ingredients.

2. Bring to the boil and skim off any surface scum with a large flat spoon.

3. Reduce the heat to a gentle simmer and cook, partially covered, for 30 minutes. Allow to cool.

4. Line a sieve (strainer) with clean muslin (cheesecloth) and place over a large jug or bowl. Pour the stock through the sieve (strainer). Discard the solids. Cover the stock and store in the refrigerator for up o 3 days until required, or eeze in small batches.

Full-fat soft cheese is rich and high in fat, but suitable substitutes can be found in skimmed milk, low-fat and reduced-fat soft cheeses. Their textures vary in softness but the flavour is mild and lends itself to sweet and savoury dishes. For savoury dishes, there are several flavoured soft cheese products – with herbs and garlic, with chives, with pineapple, etc. – which make perfect fillings for baked potatoes and omelettes.

Fromage frais is a light, fresh French cheese and has the consistency of a thick yogurt. It has a refreshing, slightly acid taste and is available in varying degrees of fat content, the lowest being a 'virtually fat-free' variety. Natural fromage frais is ideal as an accompaniment to sweet and savoury foods, and makes a perfect ingredient in sauces and dressings. Fruit-flavoured varieties are also available but although the fat content is low, check the sugar content – they are often over-sweet and more expensive. It is much better to add fruit to natural fromage frais yourself.

Mozzarella is an Italian soft cheese which melts easily and has the famous stringy texture. It is very mild in flavour and soft in texture and the fat content is suitably low. Danish Mozzarella and Mozzarella made from buffalo milk are richer, firmer and higher in fat.

Ricotta is another soft Italian cheese which can be low or medium in fat content. It has a creamy, fresh taste and can be used in sweet and savoury dishes.

Crème fraîche

Traditionally this was a rich soured cream with a fat content of between 30% and 47%, which makes it unsuitable for the low-fat diet. Now there are lower-fat varieties with a fat content of around 15% which can be included in the diet as a special treat to accompany desserts.

Cornflour (cornstarch)

An excellent thickener which can be used instead of the traditional fat–flour roux thickener to keep the fat down. Mix one part of cornflour (cornstarch) with two parts water to form a paste, then stir into soups, casseroles and sauces, and heat, stirring, until thickened.

Low-fat spread

A good substitute for butter and margarine as a spread for bread and bakery products. These spreads contain about half the calories of butter and margarines, but are also available with different fat contents. Their high water content makes them more difficult to cook with than normal cooking fats, but careful melting over a low heat will give successful results.

Milk

Choose skimmed milk when on a low-fat diet, as practically all the fat has been removed. The fat-soluble vitamins A and D are then replaced. For a creamier texture in baking and sauces, skimmed milk powder can be used with skimmed milk to enrich the recipe without greatly increasing the fat content.

Nuts and seeds

These should be used sparingly in the low-fat diet as their fat content is high. They are valuable sources of proteins and minerals, and they do provide interesting flavours in recipes. Try to avoid serving more than 15 g/½ oz per portion in any one recipe.

Coconut has a higher saturated fat content than other nuts, so it is worth avoiding it altogether in desiccated or fresh, creamed or block forms. To get the flavour it is best to make your own coconut milk or use the water from the centre of the coconut.

Sesame seeds have a rich, nutty flavour and can be made into an oily paste called tahini. This paste should be used sparingly as the fat content is high, but the flavour is so intense that a little goes a long way. It is available from health shops and delicatessens.

Oils

The use of cooking oil should be kept to a minimum. For a mild flavour choose sunflower oil, which is high in the healthier polyunsaturated fats. For stronger flavours choose olive oil or nut oils like walnut or hazelnut.

Pasta, noodles, pulses and grains

These can be used successfully in the low-fat diet to 'bulk' out dishes. They are low in fat and have a high carbohydrate content. Stir cooked brown rice into soups and casseroles to thicken, or mix one part red lentils with three parts lean minced (ground) beef to make a smaller amount of meat go further – they are virtually undetectable at this ratio. Some pastas and noodles are enriched with egg, so avoid these types where possible and look out for wholemeal (whole wheat) or rice varieties.

Stock

It is a good idea to make your own stock where possible. Some recipes for homemade stocks are provided on these pages. Ready-made stock available from shops is often very high in salt and artificial flavours which will dominate whatever dish you are preparing. This is especially true of stock that comes in cube-form. Some supermarkets do sell fresh stocks in tubs but this is an expensive convenience, although the product is very good.

Vegetables

Most are naturally low in fat and, like cereals and grains, are good for making a low-fat meal more satisfying. Grated root vegetables and finely chopped mushrooms are excellent ingredients to add to minced (ground) meats to make them go further without giving too much flavour.

Yogurt

There are many varieties of yogurt all with varying fat content from around 10% right down to 1%. Yogurt is mostly made from cows' milk, but sheeps' milk and soya-based varieties are also available. Use natural low-fat yogurt in the low-fat diet. It is made from skimmed or low-fat milk which has been fermented. It has a slightly sharp, fresh taste and is an excellent base for salad dressings and dips, or for stirring into sweet and savoury dishes or as an accompaniment. Low-fat flavoured yogurt is a good standby for a quick pudding, although you ought to check the sugar content as this can be high.

RECIPE NUTRITIONAL ANALYSES

The calorie/kilojoule and fat contents of the recipes in this book do not include any ingredients used for garnishing, serving or accompaniment.

INDEX